A Form of Expression-Signs of the Time

Cameron Weissberg

ISBN:-10:1719359202
ISBN-13:978-1719359207

We dedicate this book to all the people in the world with hardships and families that care. I also dedicate this book to my children, Logan and Alana who are contributing authors.

ACKNOWLEDGMENTS

We would like to acknowledge all the people that let me take their photos
for a small donation.

PAPER
RECYCLING
MEXICAN
WALL
FUND
PIC $1 SELFIE $2
WHAT
HAPPENED
HILLARY
RODHAM
CLINTON

Trying to smoke
some weed and
get High!!!
Spare
$1.00
Respect the
HOLLA!
Real

Justin Beiber
Stole my car and smoked
all my medical Marijanna and then
got my wifer pregnant and
then he killed my dog
Please Help

Donald Trump
is an ugly Liar
& a Crazy
BUM

TRUMP
DRUMPF
The more Lies
So much Fascist

HELLO, Like I'm Homeless!!
Like, I NEED your HELP!! Like,
AnyThing HELP's Like AT ALL!! Like
I'm Looking For A JoB!! Like No
ONE will Hire ME!! Like, Can
you Like, HELP ME!! Like, THank
you!! Like GoD BLESS you!! :)
PLEASE Help!!
Being Homeless is No Joke!!
Like You sHould HELP ouT!!
UMM! "REALLY" OMG!!

STRANDEd. DOWN
ON MY LUCK ANd
LONELY ANYTHING HELPS
EVEN SMILES. NY THANK YOU
Avenue, New York

HOMELESS WITH CANCER
PLEASE HELP,
SINCE I WAS DIAGNOSED WITH →
CLL (CHRONIC Lymphocytic LEUKEMIA)
I have BEEN UNABLE to WORK ANYMORE
I'VE APPLIED FOR SSD WAS DENIED AND
AM WAITING ON APPEAL (I HIRED AN ATTORNEY
THIS TIME)
IN THE MEANTIME I HAVE NOTHING TO LIVE
ON. Really!
THANK YOU
OLD NAVY
MANHATTAN
NY

ilestation
HIV
Positive
NEED HELP BADLY.

HOMLESS
ALONE AND IN A
ROUGH POT. ANYTHING
HELPS
HOMLESS
AND ALONE/HUNGRY!!
ANYTHING AT ALL THAT
YOU COULD SPARE WILL
GO DIRECTLY TOWARDS ME
BEING ABLE TO SLEEP INSIDE
TONIGHT. THANK YOU. GOD BLESS
GOD
LOVES
YOU

DUANEreade™
OPEN24hrs
HOMELESS. ONLY 22.
NOT FROM NYC.
TRYING TO GET ON MY FEET
HAPPY MOTHERS DAY!

HOMELESS...
BLAH BLAH
BLAH!
THANKS!

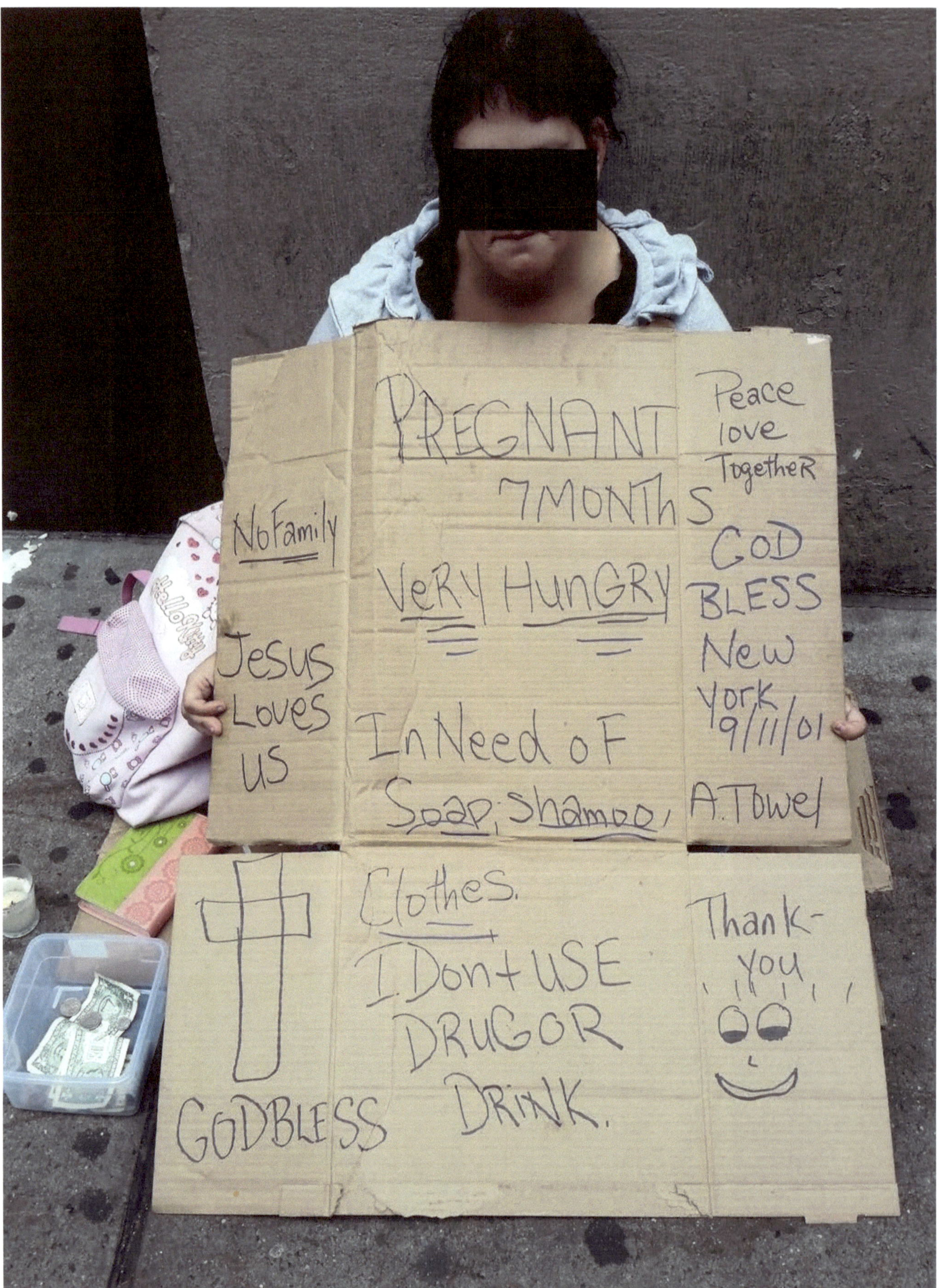
No Family
Jesus Loves US
PREGNANT 7 MONThS
VeRy HunGRy
In Need oF Soap, Shampoo,
Clothes.
I. Don+ USE DRUG OR DRINK.
Peace love Together
COD BLESS New york 9/11/01
A. Towel
Thank-you
GOD BLESS

WARM COUNT DOWN
IF 50 PEOPLE WERE
KIND ENOUG TO DONATE
JUST 1 DOLLAR... I WOULD BE
ABLE TO GET A WARM, SAFE
PLACE TO SLEEP AND SHOWER!!!
ANYTHING IS A BLESSING!!!
THANK YOU!!!

HOMLESS
HONGry
HeLP TANKS

Please Help!!!

Don't worry
about me —
pray for
Alex Rodriguez

HOMELESS, I DONT NEED MY WHOLE FAMILY, AND ALL OF MY FREINDS, OR A PARADE OF PAID IDIOTS TO PROVE IM HONEST. ONLY A PERSON NOT SURE OF HIS SELF OR A LYER WOULD NEED ALL OF THIS. ALL I NEED IS TO KEEP TELLING THE TRUTH AND LET JESUS TAKE CARE OF — THE REST.
N.Y. Urban Professionals Basketball
NYC
HOMELESS, PLEASE

PLEASE HELP!
PREGNANT + HUNGRY!
TRYING TO RAISE
$50 FOR MY ROOM +
NECESSITIES!
ANYTHING YOU COULD
SPARE IS APPRECIATED!!
Thank + God
You + Bless!
LOOK
kate spade NEW YORK

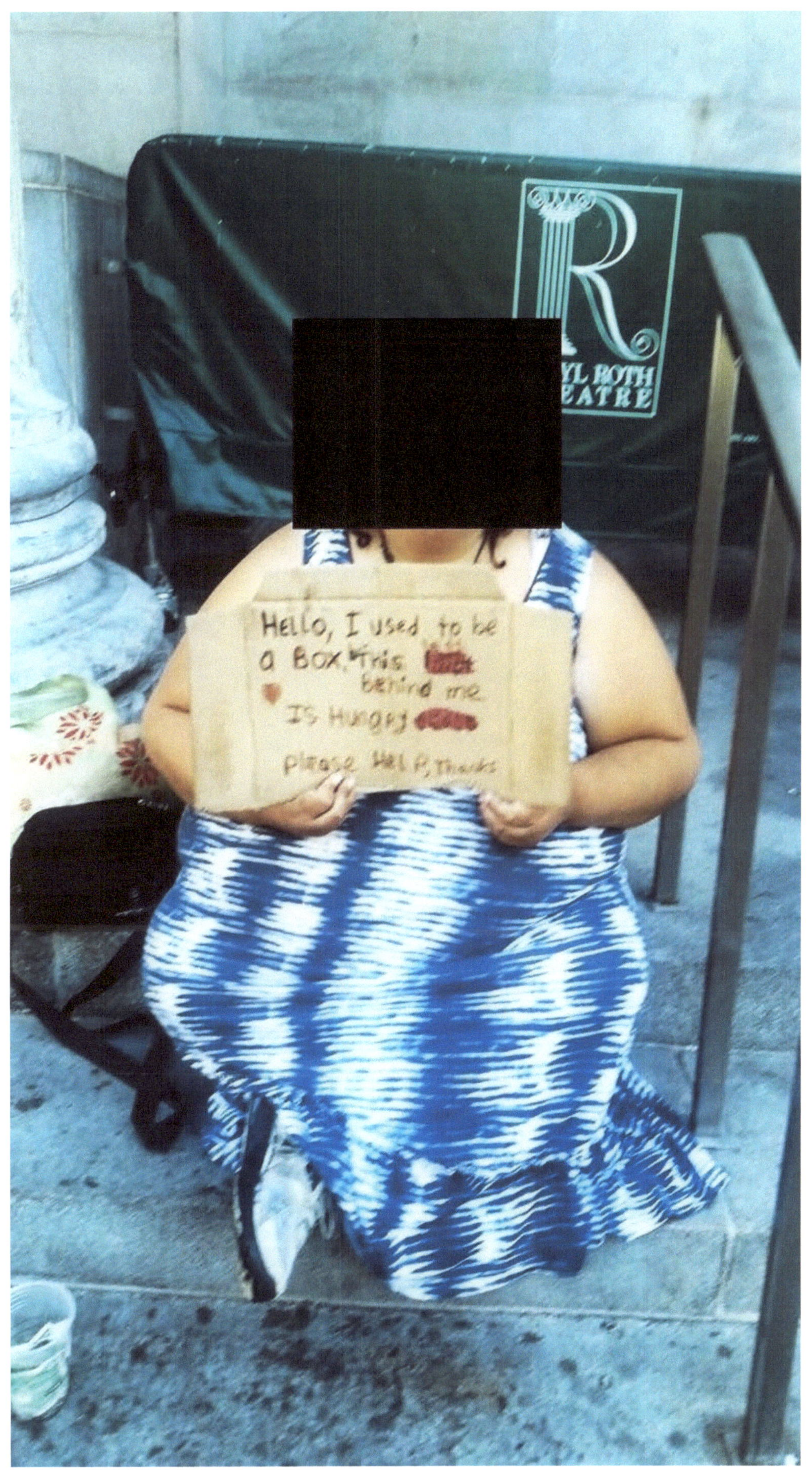
R
CHERYL ROTH
THEATRE
Hello, I used to be
a Box. This
behind me
IS Hungry
please HelP, Thanks

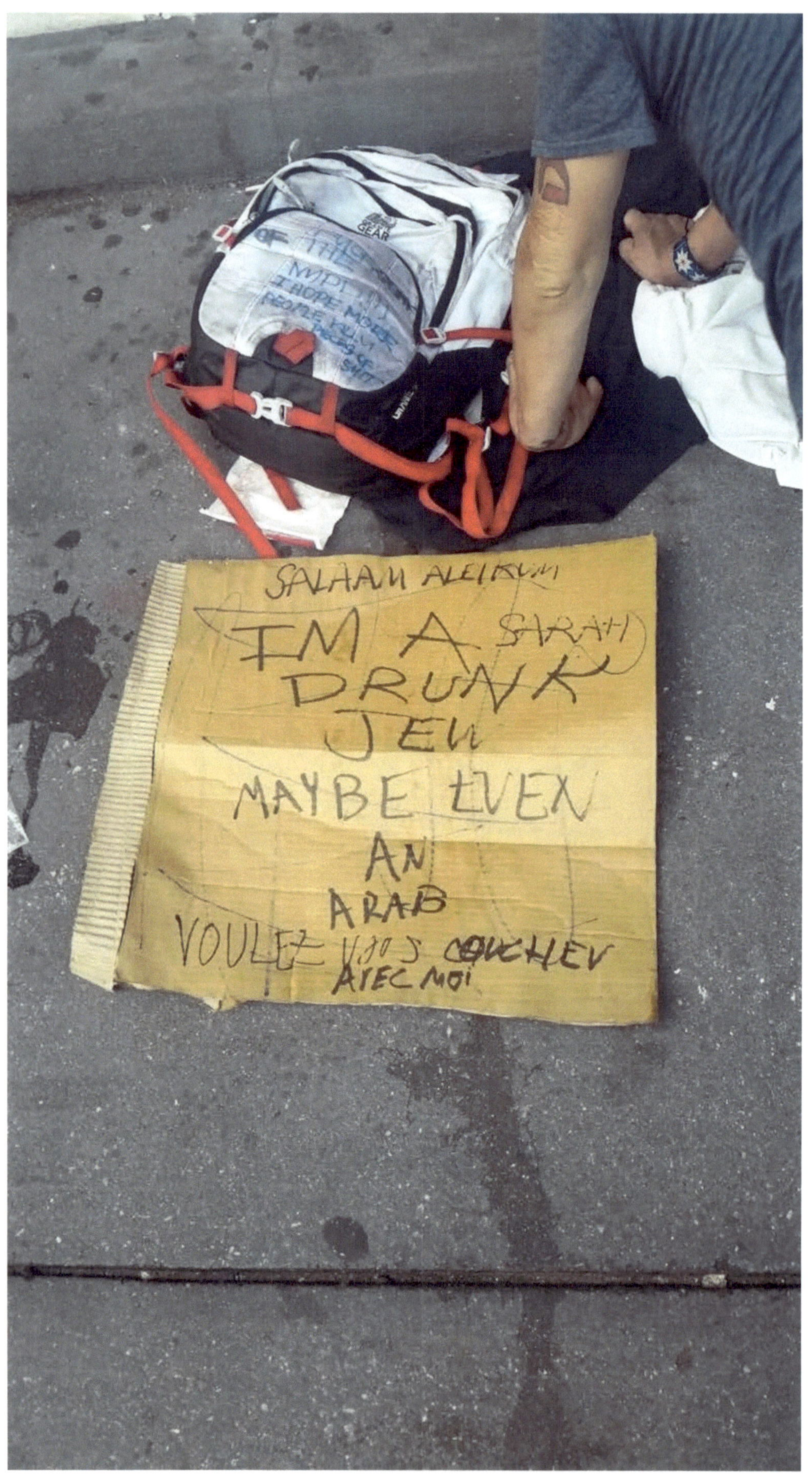
SALAAM ALEIKUM
I'M A (SARAH)
DRUNK
JEW
MAYBE EVEN
AN
ARAB
VOULEZ VOUS COUCHER
AVEC MOI

SIDEWALK
Support The
of Vehicles
STEAMROLLERS
Never
Give UP
trying   to   get   Some
DINNER
Please   spare   Whatever
You can.
God Bless
YOU

Any Bit Of
Kindness
Helps...
anything helps
SMILE...
Have A
Wonderful
Day!!
Thank You & God Bless

Lost my Job
And APT. ANY
HELP IS
APPRECIATED
THANK you. God bless

4 1/2 MONTHS PREGNANT
HOMELESS AND HUNGRY
PLEASE ANYTHING HELPS
FOOD
DRINKS MATERNAL GIFT CARDS THANK
BABY ITEMS YOU GOD
CLOTHES CHANGE/A DOLLAR BLESS
4 1/2 MONTHS PREGNANT
HUNGRY AND HOMELESS
PLEASE HELP
THANK YOU
GOD
BLESS
FOOD/DRINKS MATERNAL GIFT CARDS
BABY STUFF
18 WEEKS PREGNANT (4 1/2 MONTHS)
HOMELESS AND HUNGRY
PLEASE HELP ANYTHING WILL
THANK YOU
GOD BLESS
FOOD/DRINKS MATERNAL
BABY ITEMS GIFT CARDS
CLOTHING CHANGE
A FEW DOLLARS

LONEINESS IS THE HARDEST PART OF HOMELESSNESS
Stop by and SAY SomeThing Nice
it HelPs AloT
* Drug * Free
DonT Pass Me BY. I So Happen To Be A Nice Guy.
So Please Stop BY Just to Say Hi
* Drug * Free *
M NOT HOMELESS because Drug and Alcohol Addictions

Dreaming
of
Bagels &
Coffee

The End

ABOUT THE AUTHOR

Cameron Weissberg has been living with her 2 children in NYC and wants to use her observations of the city's homeless to bring awareness and promote change.